JOURNEY TO LONDON

A Love story about second chances

By

Monet Love-Peterson
&
Lawrence Peterson

A memoir

Printed in the United States of America Lulu Press

Morrisville, NC

First time printing: February 2021

ISBN 978-1-736-2209-0-0

molove.shop

MONET'S CHAPTERS

1. North Carolina A&T..3

2. Becoming a Mommy..11

3. Migrating South..21

4. Paying the Price - Lesson not Learned.............................31

5. Begin Again...43

6. Obedience brings a reward...53

7. London- Our answered prayer..63

LARRY'S CHAPTERS

1. North Carolina A&T..7

2. Atlanta "ATL"..17

3. Home Bound..29

4. Single Again...39

5. Yellow Brick Road..49

6. Love at First Sight...59

7. London - Our answered prayer...69

Journey to London

A Love story about
second chances

By

Monet Love-Peterson
&
Lawrence Peterson

A memoir

INTRODUCTION

Every step of our life journey, past and present has a purpose. God never wastes an experience, relationship, test, trial or triumph. As it states in Romans 8:28 He works everything together for our good. Who knew that someone I met 30 years prior, hung out and danced with, never dated, and couldn't even remember his face (even after reconnecting with him) would end up being my husband and making me the happiest lady in the world?? God knew!

This is truly a love story about patience and God's Divine Time! A destiny moment led to a beautiful path which we pray will encourage others. Anyone who has been divorced, starting over after a bad break up or never married before but still "TRUSTING GOD" for your Boaz, we pray that our love story will remind you that God has not forgotten! He hears your prayers. He has it all mapped out. Are you open to His best? Are you listening? Your potential mate may be someone you already know. Don't go looking ladies, he'll find you. He who finds a wife finds a good thing, and obtains favor from the Lord. Proverbs 18:22

I pray that my sisters in their 40's and 50's have their spiritual eyes open. Money, cars, a handsome face, topped off with a plump 401K may appear essential or even necessary when you're dangling outside the door of retirement. However, too often extremely wealthy men saddled with titles and status use their money and prestige to Lord over their spouse, or the counterfeit "representative" shows up and over time you learn that the potential knight in shining armor was a counterfeit. Time and accountability have a beautiful way of revealing the truth. Are you willing to submit even at 45 years old? You may overlook what the world considers lowly and average career, but THIS firefighter, my husband and King, is the kindest and most gentle spirited man who dons that gear. Each day he heads out to rescue people from danger but he is MY everyday hero! He was and still is an amazing gentleman. Larry is the most patient loving soul I have ever been blessed to know and now I call him my husband.

North Carolina A&T SU

(Monet)

I am no stranger to hard work. While in High school I had three jobs. I worked at Laces skating rink, delivered newspapers on the weekends, and my favorite job was at the local animal shelter called the North Shore Animal League. Everyone who knew me believed that I would be a veterinarian, and I wanted to attend an HBCU (Historically Black College/University). So, when it came time to apply for colleges in my Senior year I naturally applied to Tuskegee, NCA&T SU, and a few colleges in Florida. Those college brochures with books on the beach were so tantalizing I quickly visualized myself studying while getting a golden bronze tan. In reality, I knew I wouldn't do much studying. So, I quickly dismissed those as options.

Becoming a veterinarian was my heart's desire, however, when I got promoted to assisting in the clinic that desire dwindled. I already smuggled stray animals into my basement without my mother knowing, but when I got attached to little puppies or

3

cats who didn't survive a surgery my heart broke and I would go home a wreck. There was no possible way I could do this daily as a job. So, I decided to do what most kids do. I chose to follow my mother's career path. She was an accountant and worked at Arthur Anderson, one of the top accounting firms in the country at that time. Then, after scanning over my life I realized two of the most successful people in my life, my Aunt Gwen and Uncle Ed, whom I deeply admired, attended and met on the campus of NCA&T SU. That was it! I would attend A&T and become an "Aggie Dog" which was their mascot and I chose to major in accounting. That one decision laid the foundation for me to meet "Largo Larry." The friend I couldn't remember, now, the love of my life.

We met and became acquaintances in the Summer of 1987, my freshman year on the campus of North Carolina A&T University. My cousin DT attended A&T and was a Senior on campus. It was great having a big cousin there to teach me the ropes and introduce me to new friends. He was also a part of Phi Beta Sigma, a black fraternity. He pledged Larry and they shared the same suite in one of the male dormitories. I met "Largo Larry" one day while going to visit my big cousin DT. He told me years later that Largo had a crush on me. I remember my cousin sharing that one day after I left their suite, Larry said "I Love her." That was such a sweet comment but I had a boyfriend and was committed to waiting by the phone booth in my dorm each night to receive his phone calls. Although DT introduced us we never dated. We hung out on campus in between classes and even partied at the BJ's 2-6am jams, but all of this was according to my cousin Shae. She recounted stories of the three of us burning up the dance floor to House and GoGo music. However, I strained and vaguely remembered these accounts. We partied with lots of people so this was not standing out in my memory. There wasn't a specific memory from which I could laugh or reflect. In fact, I had absolutely no recollection whatsoever of Larry aka "Largo". Probably because my tenure at A&T was short lived and my life and mindset changed drastically after I left. My mother tried hard to keep me there, but being a single mother and paying all the bills in the house she bought for us in Port Washington, Long Island was a lot to handle. The tuition payments tipped the scale and it wasn't in my favor. Her inability to make the tuition payments along with a tumultuous life of abuse she endured from her boyfriend left me packing my bags and returning home to New York. I made lots of friends in NC. Shae was my roadie. We partied, traveled, and had our own apartment in Greensboro. Those were two of the most fun years of my life. And also the last years of being a teen or living a single life as I knew it. I left A&T two years later and began another chapter in my life. That was 25 years ago.

NORTH CAROLINA AGRICULTURAL AND TECHNICAL STATE UNIVERSITY

(Larry)

I was a somewhat shy, skinny kid from Largo Maryland by way of Suitland MD, Buffalo NY, and Washington DC. Entering my freshman year at NCA&TSU, I quickly realized that my life growing up was preparation for me on my own. I attended eight different schools before I graduated from high school. A constant move to survive with a single parent mom and one sibling is what led me to these schools, a blessing in disguise. All the moving helped me with meeting new people. It was the fall of 1985, there I was figuring out what to wear for my first day and the gear I had was paraphernalia from high school. So I thought that was a good idea to let people know where I come from. Little did I know wearing a jacket, sweatshirt, T shirts and a very deserving class ring all reading LARGO LIONS would lead to my campus nickname. At Largo we were coming off of a State championship (track), and because I wore something that said Largo on it everyday or almost everyday that would begin to form a lifelong nickname Largo Larry or just "LARGO". My very first roommate was also from Largo High school. We had planned this after finding out we both had decided to attend A&T. He too, was proud of where we came from however, the nickname LARGO, became my badge that I wear to this day.

While I was in a college town, and roaming the "streets" of campus I met a lot of new people, one being my best friend to this day Will, his nickname was III (third). I also met Chad or (Chilly) as he preferred. These two and I met in the parking lot of the Moore gym on the outside basketball court. We were all shorter and a lot younger looking than our peers. We played several fast paced somewhat physical games of 21. The recollection as to who won is vague and biased. In hindsight we all won because we are all still friends, over thirty years later. This was one of the best things about college, you meet lifelong friends that are with you long after you leave.

It was in the fall of 1987, I stayed in Haley Hall, a dormitory named after Alex Haley, the great author that wrote Roots. In this dorm we had suites with four rooms to a suite, a communal bathroom containing two showers and two toilets. All that to say you basically had seven roommates. In my suite, we housed a mixed group of the student body, some were freshmen and some upperclassmen. I was a rising junior credit wise, however like a lot of people, I was in the midst of a change of major and still trying to discover what I wanted to do with my life. Ultimately, I spent six years at good old A&T. Although it took longer than a typical four year period for me to decide on a major and graduate I don't recommend spending your money this way. Anyway, Darryl (DT) was one of my suitemates and visiting him on several occasions was his cousin Monet and her close friend Shae-la-fa both french if you would have asked me. I developed a crush on Monet but kept it to myself only expressing it to Darryl after they would leave. Monet had a boyfriend and she let it be known, all while being nice and a little flirty. Now, because they visited often we became friends and started hanging out on different occasions, but mainly at parties on the dance floor. Because I felt like I couldn't tell her how I "really" felt about her, the dance floor was where I could express myself best. I was crushed when two years later I found out she had left school for unknown reasons. I decided in my later years to pledge and join a fraternity. I was very selective in the brotherhood and Greek organization that I would represent. Darryl, being older than me with influence, helped in my decision to join the most prestigious organization and men of distinction which is Phi Beta Sigma. We stand for brotherhood, scholarship and service. I pledged in the Spring of 1990 and was number six out of twelve and honcho which meant the leader of my line. DT and I became frat brothers. I always asked him about Monet and inquired about how and what she

9

was doing, not really finding out anything other than she was fine the last time he saw her.

As I continued my years at A&T, I eventually discovered my vision for a major which was Communications. I grew as a person and discovered more about myself. I wasn't the quiet little skinny kid that first walked onto campus. I developed into a young man who was gregarious and outgoing. I was willing to try new things. I gained broadcast communications skills by becoming a radio DJ on campus in charge of the "Love Zone." I love music and enjoyed playing ballads and songs that led my generation into the Love zone. I joined the cheering squad and became a stuntman. I quickly became co-captain and loved hyping up the crowds during our infamous football and basketball games. Finally, I was also the "Aggie Dog" which is A&T's mascot. I became more popular, developed confidence, and made a lot of life long friends and acquaintances. I graduated in 1991 with a BS in Broadcast Communications and a minor in Theater Technology. This became one of the greatest times, seasons and best memories of my life. I am forever an A&T AGGIE . (Aggie Pride).

BECOMING A MOMMY

(Monet)

I jumped right back into a college classroom upon my return to New York. Of course, that was right after I kicked my mother's boyfriend and his sons out of our house. They were running our home and her car into the ground. I was accustomed to my mother allowing the men in her life to treat her horribly. Taking her money, gambling, drinking and then physical abuse. This was a pattern and she seemed to choose the same exact type of man at each turn. She really knew how to pick them. Or, I suppose they knew how to "spot" her. My mother was the sweetest kindest lady I have ever met and I adored her, but I spent all of my childhood and most of my adult life protecting her and speaking up for her until she went to rest in the Masters arms. My mom was adopted and she explained that going from foster home to foster home made her feel unwanted. I didn't understand at first but later as I got older, matured a bit, became a mother, but most importantly gave my life to Christ, I finally understood her level of pain. Once I began studying and understanding the scriptures, I realized that my mother was on a quest for love. Love from her parents, Love from a man, acceptance from her peers and a deep longing THIRST that ONLY Christ the living God could quench. That revelation occurred to me as I continued to develop a deeper relationship with God. However, I didn't get saved until 1995 when my son was five. I spent most of that in between time being angry with her and her lifestyle. I was angry with her for drinking her problems away which were always there waiting at the door for her the next morning. I was angry at the men who used and abused her, and sadness masked in anger that my dad never came around to help her. I was angry but I wasn't mean. I was kind and giving just like my mother and because I wasn't raised by my father I had no idea that I got my gregarious personality from him. However, since my mother raised me her personality influenced me most and I was determined with every fiber in my being to be a strong outspoken lady that would never let anyone treat me like trash. I figured in life they may try, but I would never be weak enough to stay with someone who didn't love me. Oh, if I only knew then, that if you just keep living long enough many of my "I would never" statements will be tested. I spent most of my life defending my mom. Now that I am back in New York I had to clean up her house once again.

It didn't take long for me to get rid of the type of men my mom would attract and this particular guy would be no different. I would quickly point out the using spirit and then they would choose to bounce. This last guy broke her arm by tossing her from the car while it was still moving and it STILL took me and my very first boyfriend (turned good friend) to convince my mother that she was worth more than what she was allowing. I don't know what Rodney said but after one conversation with that clown he and his sons stopped coming around.

I enrolled in the Spring semester at Borough of Manhattan Community College so my mind and face could stay in a book while waiting to get accepted to Pace University also in Manhattan. While taking classes at BMCC I met my son's father and after a short dating period I was pregnant. Petrified! Here I was 20 years old and scared to death because I remember my mother's story. She got pregnant at 20 and back in those times young girls were "sent away" to unwed mothers homes. So, she was sent away. When I told her that I was pregnant she was furious. She was watching her daughter repeat her same mistake and she would not stand for it. She insisted that I get an abortion or get married. I screamed back with passion "I'm not getting married, I don't even know him well enough to marry him" I heard myself. It was loud. But on the inside I was saying to myself, "How could I open my legs and let someone in and not know them well enough to marry them?" Yikes! This was ugly. I was ugly. I didn't like myself too much at that moment. I remember feeling so stupid. My son's father was a great guy. He actually said to my mother right there, "I'll marry Monet". I quickly rebuffed " No you won't! We weren't talking about marriage before". Besides, I was smart

13

enough to know that babies don't make people stay together. My mother insisted that I get an abortion because I wasn't going to embarass her living in our "all white neighborhood" and people see my belly growing and no ring on my finger. I told her, "No, I'm not going to do it". However, after much persuasion my son's father and I went to Manhattan to an abortion clinic. That day changed my life for the REST of my life.

We took the train together in silence knowing that it will be over in a few hours, the death of the baby and the death of our relationship. We exited the train station, took the escalator up, entered an office building and filled out paperwork. They called me back to give a blood and urine sample to confirm that I was indeed pregnant. Then they asked for the payment which we provided and then I was escorted into a back room. Then the unexplainable happened. I heard what I believed was an audible voice say "Get up and leave, I will take care of you." Then I heard it a second time. I was paralyzed. My mother took my brother and I to church every weekend of our lives but I had NEVER heard God speak to me. Was that God? Is that what he sounds like? The next voice I heard was a lady saying come right this way, you're next. Again, paralyzed. I couldn't move. The lady repeated it to which I replied "I'm keeping my baby!" She then stated that it will be over quickly. So, I repeated my statement, "I am keeping my baby." "Good for you," she replied. I ran from the back and told Monty's dad I could not do it. I went to a nearby payphone and called my mother and told her I could not go through with it and that I was keeping my baby. She screamed to the top of her lungs for me to go back upstairs and have the abortion. I screamed back NO! She then told me that I have got to get out of her house. Montys's Dad and I barely spoke on the train all the way back home. While the realities of motherhood and fatherhood were racing through our minds someone walking through the subway cars began passing out tracks. They were Christian pamphlets with a different topic on each. The one he handed to me was the picture of a baby in a mother's stomach on the front with the words that are forever etched in my mind. "God Loves the unborn." Now, I KNEW that was God that spoke to me and my life was forever changed.

I went back to Long Island, packed my bags and moved out of my mother's house and in with my foster grandmother, the lady who raised my mother. When my mother returned from the unwed mothers home she lived in while pregnant with me, she was empty handed. She explained that she had given me to the facility so that I could be placed up for adoption. My foster grandfather, Grandpa Whitehall told my mother to go back and get me and that they would help her. Here my mom was once again reliving her past choices now in my life. Deja vu is something else. She couldn't stand the shame and ridicule. I am so grateful for the hearts of the Whitehalls. We also had the support of my son's other grandmother. She was and still is a powerful, strong yet gentle woman of God. She was extremely supportive and I am eternally grateful for her tender words and offering of support in that frightening season. However, my safe place was with the Whitehalls. We stayed there throughout my entire pregnancy. The same beautiful brownstone house that fostered my mother and her two older sisters in Bedford Stuyvesant, Brooklyn, New York was the peaceful haven Monty and I lived for several months before making the move south and turning the next chapter of our lives. We had pampers stacked from the floor to the ceiling and round-the-clock visitors bringing us food and tons of Love. God was indeed faithful to perform his word to me. "Get up and leave, I will take care of you." That HE did.

My mother was so ashamed that she did not even call me until Monty was four months old. She was looking in a mirror and felt embarrassed by MY choice to keep MY baby. Once she looked into the beautiful brown eyes of her first grandson she fell deeply in love and sobbed uncontrollably. I forgave her quickly for I knew she lived a life of "people pleasing" and fearful of what "they" would say. I was different in that way. I was charting my own path. Making tons of mistakes but strong enough to tell my own mother, "no." Little did I know my life was about to change again. This change would test all the life skills I gained during my childhood. Being a mommy put everything to the test. Would I pass?

16

ATL

(Lawrence)

I left A&T but I did not leave Greensboro NC. I had several jobs. I was still working at the television station, working a temporary job with the post office, and part timer for American Express. I was happy to graduate but I knew that Greensboro wasn't my final stop. The post office job was temporary and was coming to an end soon. Therefore, it felt like a natural time for a change. Chad and I had been to Atlanta several times in the past. Once for Martin Luther King holiday, other times just to travel with friends to a nearby city that was on the rise to "Hotlanta" status. We liked Atlanta so much we decided to move there and give the music industry a shot. Chad had already been working with different groups he put together with some family and friends, and I thought I could be of some help in the area of choreography. Yes, I thought I could dance. In fact, I knew I could dance. I just needed the right opportunity. January 1994 came and I was ready to go. However, you know things couldn't happen that easy, Chad wasn't ready, so I moved with another Aggie Alum, my big Sister Renee. She was already living there and didn't hesitate to offer me her home. Framily (Friends like Family) is great. Found a job to make ends meet and was off and running. Chad eventually made it down and we stayed in the nearby hotel for a week, until we got our own apartment. We were working so much, trying to find room for music wasn't that easy. In the meantime, at least five additional friends migrated to Atlanta and lived with us until 1997. I decided to throw myself a 30th birthday bash and move out on my own. Now on my own, I was still doing what someone had done for me. Offering my place to other "framily" making the move and transition to Atlanta.

Lots of things changed this year. I started dating someone exclusively. I was working at Hot 97 in the traffic dept, back when Ludacris was known as Chris luva luva. I had gone to an audition for the Atlanta Hawks dance and cheer squad because that year they were adding men. Like I said I thought I could dance, until I realized very quickly that jazz dance was also dancing and not my finest two step. Needless to say, I didn't make that team. However, while at that audition I saw another framily member who did make the team and was doing very well in the world of dance. His name was Chuck Maldonaldo. Chuck and I stayed in touch and he later called me about joining a hip-hop dance group that performed during Battle of the Bands. This was a big event held in Atlanta each year. After doing that for two years, Chuck became the Choreographer for Left Eye, and had a country wide audition to join that team. I auditioned and made that team. While performing around Atlanta with this new team of dancers, we all stuck together practicing the routines we learned from Chuck in anticipation that we would be the dancers for TLC on tour for the up and coming album. Well that didn't pan out, for reasons unbeknownst to us. We remained Left Eye production dancers, and audition opportunities for other artists came about. The next thing you know, there I was dancing for different artists while still trying to work my regular 9 to 5. This business was so much fun and lucrative that I quit the 9 to 5 or in my case the 11pm to 7am to pursue it full time. Here I am 32 yrs young and doing something that I envisioned four years prior to moving to the ATL, only my vision was much smaller than God's plans. Now a year into this transition I also became involved with a woman whom I would date longer than anyone else. We dated for nine months. After two years of living an exciting career for me, my world as I knew it began to break down. My father, despite his choices in life to leave my mother with two kids my sister(5) and I (7), found out at 60yrs old he had a rare condition found in adults. A spinal tumor which had grown around his spine like a snake, undetected for years. While waiting on a specialist to do the surgery, my father developed an infection from bed sores which led to sepsis. My family began telling me it was time to come home. By the time I reached the hospital I realized my father was already gone and was being kept alive by the hospital machines, and because I was his oldest child it was left up to me to decide his fate. Although we were father and son, the relationship was not a bond, it was one of acknowledgement for each others' title. My father's destiny was already determined by God and my decision to keep him alive for as long as his body would last was nothing but a selfish gesture for myself and the rest of my family. My father passed away, not even thirty minutes after making my decision. This was September of 2000. This became a very important time in my life, because my mother had gotten ill the year before and these major life changes concerning my parents made me re-evaluate the course of my life.

Migrating South

(Monet)

When I see a door I knock and go inside. We never know what blessing is waiting for us if we fearlessly walk. Being raised as a latchkey kid in Brooklyn New York and having countless responsibilities made me pretty fearless at a young age. Many of our blessings will come through the people in our lives. Someone will open a door for us and we need to "carpe diem" which means seize the moment. My sister Donna has opened up many doors for me. Doing something new and different was extremely appealing and so was gaining some independence. It is because of my big sister D that I have made northern Virginia my home and have a plethora of priceless gems in my life that I call friends and family because of that decision.

Soon after crossing the stage and receiving my high school diploma my sister told me of a receptionist position at her employment that needed to be filled as soon as possible. So, I jumped. I packed my belongings left NYC at seventeen years old and moved to Alexandria Virginia and stayed with her and her growing family. This was the hot Summer of 1987 BEFORE I went to NC A&T. She taught me priceless lessons on how to save for college and helped me to purchase all the necessities before diving to college and officially on my own. It was also in that Summer that I walked into a drug store and met a wonderful young man who swept me off my feet. He treated me like a lady. He was chivalrous and generous. This was life changing and eye opening because this was the VERY first time anyone had ever treated me with such love. I witnessed my mother giving and giving but I never observed a man, ANY MAN treat her with the respect and love I found myself receiving. Was this even possible? My father didn't raise me. I don't have one single memory of waking up and seeing my dad cook breakfast or even knew what a daily routine with a man in the home would be like. Normal for me was abuse. I had no expectations from a man other than to protect myself, speak up and be clear that I would be no one's punching bag. Is this what love looks like? I was clueless and couldn't recognize love staring me right in the face. I know NOW that love is a verb and this young man was not playing. THIS is the reason I left for college two months later with all my college dreams, hopes, wishes and a boyfriend. That's why I did go out and party and enjoyed my college life experiences, but I also sat outside that pay phone waiting for it to ring. We were inseparable, as much as a distant relationship could allow. This is the main reason I did not give "Largo Larry" or any other young man on my college campus much weight or consideration. My heart and mind were set on making this relationship outlast the distance. Youth and immaturity have a way of taking us off course or a path we did not intend.

Once I left NC A&T and back in the Big Apple I quickly registered and began college classes at the community college in Manhattan. The long distant relationship which kept me content in college was too difficult to sustain. The space became greater than all the love deposits we made in the past. I decided to sever that distant relationship and not long after the gift of motherhood was sitting in my lap. I only dated my son's father a few months. This was not our plan. I was petrified. This baby was the gift I didn't know I needed or wanted. My next chapter was raising the beautiful son that God had given me and that wonderful gentleman from my past had become a casualty of space, and a distant memory. So, I thought. When I moved back to the DMV where I originally met the "gentleman" a true heart effort was made to rekindle what was lost. However, the irreversible blows to our trust coupled with the emotional hurt had us continuously spiraling downward in confusion and frustration. We relinquished our former titles and pressed forward to salvage the friendship. I was growing up and making grown up choices. Our choices are long lasting and life changing.

The truth is once I decided to keep my son I thought "I'm going to make this new relationship work and lie in the bed I made" that didn't work. We were young, afraid and barely knew

23

one another. We tried but quickly learned the critical lesson that babies don't make people stay together, especially if there wasn't a solid foundation and substance prior to the pregnancy. When Monty was six months old I packed our belongings and migrated south back to Alexandria Virginia. We moved in with my sister once again for a few months and then on to our very own space.

Our first home together as mommy and son was located in Washington DC. It was a small efficiency apartment humbly furnished with three pieces of furniture, his crib, table and chairs and a couch which turned into my bed. It was perfect. It was ours. The best part about this move was that the Woodner had a childcare facility located on the lower level and they had a spot for my baby boy. To top off the blessings it cost me one dollar to take the bus each way to work and back each day! God is good. I remember praying one time when my money was stretched and my broke was broke, "God help me make it to my next paycheck!". He answered me and it was just enough light for the next step. Another time, my cousin Shae mailed me ten dollars because God laid me on her heart. That was my carfare to work and back for a week until my next paycheck. Look at God! He was faithful and he held up to what he spoke to me in the abortion clinic that day, he would take care of me. Jehovah Jireh, he was our provider.

I changed employment and that allowed Monty and I to move back to Alexandria Virginia a few years later. Along our journey we shared apartments with different relatives who migrated to

Virginia like my cousin Marne and cousin Lashae who was like a second mother to Monty. We helped and supported others the same way my sister Donna supported us. I wouldn't change any part of the journey. All the relationships, love interests, broken hearts and tears were power for the course. It's all preparation. Monty and I were living in our own place and had a nice comfortable routine and then a man knocked on our door. Well, he knocked on my door. The door of my heart and that changed both our lives in every way imaginable. He wasn't a complete stranger but I only knew of him through my mother. I did not know him personally. His name is Jesus.

Monty was five years old. I met him in the lower level of a hotel building in a church called Agape Embassy. The pastor was a sharp, wise man full of wisdom. He was also very hard, direct, and a straight shooter. He never sugar coated the truth to pacify your feelings. Feelings, what's that?? I was in his office with a wonderful man who I was in a relationship with and we were living together, but not getting along very well. This was our shot to get some help or advice. Well, something. Neither of us truly knew how drastic this would alter our lives. The Pastor asked me a simple but strange question that was mind altering, because I knew the answer immediately. Years later, I have asked tons of young women trying to navigate their way around in the world and develop their relationship with the Lord the same set of questions. Many of us try to tap dance in the gray areas of life because we can, or because in choosing we feel like we

25

may lose somebody we think we want to keep. The question provides absolutely no room for grey. **"Can you be a little bit pregnant?"** No, you're either pregnant or you're not, and you can't be a little bit married, you're either married or you're not. He then turned and said to me, you never want your son to remember his mother lying in a bed with a man that's not her husband. Well, that straight shooter shot hit me square between the eyes and heart. My son meant more to me than Jesus at that time because I hadn't surrendered to Christ. He was still a visitor, but that was changing. God knows EXACTLY what it will take to get his children's attention and obedience. We moved, the guy I was living with moved, and our lives shifted and we took an elevator slowly up a long building called salvation. I made a ton of mistakes. I was hungry for the Word of God but didn't have any knowledge. I was thirsty and eager to learn. Often new believers are zealous and excited by the Joy that comes with gaining Christ, but Oh, was I judgemental. I could easily recognize the faults in others far easier than in myself but, I was still committed to learning. This walk with Christ is a journey and that young man and our growing pains cost us that relationship. However, I know that our God makes no mistakes and I wasn't ready for the commitment of marriage, let alone learn the potential and the power in singleness. Learning the priceless lesson that you must be **"whole" BEFORE you get married** is a painful but profitable class in life most of us skip. This major component in singleness confuses so many young people. We run around looking for someone to "complete us" and end up hurting ourselves and our potential partner. Short cutting knowledge is a disaster waiting to happen and leaves a string of broken hearts. I was learning to work out my salvation with fear and trembling, but surrender, well that takes a lifetime. I didn't know what tomorrow holds, but I was learning who holds tomorrow.

I'm grateful to say Pastor Mills teachings still remain in my heart and spirit to this day. Countless people have been blessed because of his sacrifice, study and arduous delivery of the word of God. His wife, Mrs. Renee was the heartbeat of the church and became a surrogate mother who taught me the word of God through her teachings. She also displayed transparency in her lessons. That would prove to be priceless to me as a teacher myself. My thirst and hunger for God's word brought an insatiable appetite unlike anything I had ever experienced in my life. Living waters were taking place in the depths of my belly and I was being transformed because my mind and heart were being massaged and nurtured. Monty and I never missed a bible study or Sunday at church. If the church doors were open we were coming through. When I chose to live my life for Christ I went IN! No drinking, no smoking, no clubbing, no secular music or anything that could possibly take me off my unwavering focus and course to grow in Christ. I had an unquenchable thirst for the word of God and found satisfaction in Him. For a season, I had no friends. My girls thought my change of heart and lifestyle was a phase. They figured I would eventually return to the club, but this was for real. My heart was sold out forever. Of course my walk had bumps, hills and valleys, but I was convinced that Jesus was the answer to the questions in my heart. I just didn't have all the answers, not all at once and certainly at 25 I didn't even know the correct questions to ask. However, I did know this, I was choosing to live for Christ. All of my life for the rest of my life. I meant that then and mean it today. Imperfect Christian that's me! Did I say I made mistakes? My spiritual journey has developed but not without COUNTLESS mistakes, snares, pitfalls and trusting in my own strength. However, no matter how many times I stumbled, the Lord would catch me with His righteous right hand. Would I be worthy of all that was to come? I was still learning.

Homebound

(Larry)

Cutting the umbilical cord is hard enough as a youth but trying to make it on your own is an even bigger challenge. Your parents worry, you are green to the world while at the same time feeling like you need your own space. Freedom…. to do what I want, when I want, and how I want. Yep. I didn't want to answer to anyone but me. So instead of asking for permission,I only need to ask for forgiveness if I did something that I knew probably wasn't the best decision for my life. I've made a lot of mistakes along the way trying to do it on my own, however the foundation my mother set for me came rumbling back like a smack you didn't see coming. This is when the internal evaluation hit me December 2000. I was making my own way out here in the world. I had a girlfriend that I had been dating for a year and a half and she was thinking about moving home to New Jersey. The dance team I was a part of was breaking up and a few of them were moving to California.

My thoughts were all over the place. I'm 33 years old, dancing background for artists for a living, in an apartment with a friend, my father's passing still fresh in my mind, my mother was sick, not completely healed, and my best friend was married two years with two kids. Boom! Everything hit me at once. I needed to be doing something more with my life. But what? I had made my decision just like that. I needed to make a commitment to this woman I was with, and find a career with benefits. Most importantly, I needed to be closer to my family. Everything pointed in one direction, moving back home to Maryland. This became a no brainer for me. In a year and a half God brought into fruition all of these things. In 2002, I got married fresh out of the fire academy, and bought a home two years later just outside of Maryland in Pennsylvania.

Paying the Price - Lesson not Learned

(Monet)

The mistake will be repeated until the lesson is learned. I don't know about my sisters out there but this sister is REAL. Real hard headed. That's how many of us are and behave until we find out who we really are. Who God says we are. I wish I could say that after I had a child outside of marriage the FIRST time, that I never had sex outside of the covenant boundaries and protection of marriage, but that wasn't the case.

Pain is often how God gets our attention. You pray harder and more fervently when you're uncomfortable. There is no time for cute patty cake prayers when your heart is aching and broke down with humiliation and pain. I know I am most prone to go to God AND listen to him when I am in pain, and He knows his daughter. Monty and I were attending church several times a week and I was committed to us growing in Christ as a family.

I was dedicated to Monty and we had a schedule that kept us on course to grow. Then several of my "sister friends" joined me and we began our own bible study. In that Sister circle we all chose to sign a commitment to dedicate ourselves to deepen our relationship with God. If we had a boyfriend we chose to put him on the back burner, tell him about this six month journey of going "under construction" with God. No men. This process would help us to individually and uniquely develop and strengthen our personal relationships with the Lord. We were holding one another accountable. Proverbs 17:17 As iron sharpens iron so one man sharpens another. We knew we needed one another, but we were such young believers that often our sharpening lacked tact and compassion. Well, definitely mine. Nevertheless, many of us remained in the circle of Love and I am proud to say, each one of them, though the relationships have been tested, they are all still my friends/sisters until this day and I try my hardest to be there whenever I am called on. This group was so essential for me because I was the loudest mouth proclaiming the call to celibacy and desiring for ALL five of us to be committed to that and I was the one to get pregnant. Yep, me and my big mouth.

As soon as our construction was over my boyfriend asked me to attend premarital classes at his church. The classes were once a month for a year. Yes, you read correctly. One whole year. Shortly after our six months of construction with my girlfriends, I was in pre-marital classes for an entire year. In the classes we had weekly homework assignments. This process required tons of

WAITING and patience. We weren't alone because there were 50 other anxious couples in our class. Patience was tested right away, because our Pastor stated in the very FIRST class, if you've been given a ring, give it back. We don't know what will be decided by the end of the class and a ring and wedding date are a distraction. I took mine off right then and handed it to my fiance. My pastor said he made the classes a year long on purpose. He continued there are a lot of wolves that come disguised in sheep's clothes, and typically, the tail will fall out within a year. AFTER a year of group lessons and assignments, he begins one on one counselling with each couple . The time frame to completion varied in time depending on their specific dynamics and spiritual maturity of each couple.

Well, my fiance was saved and also committed to Christ, but he began pressing me to have intercourse. I eventually yielded and got pregnant. We needed to ask for permission to remain in the class, which was granted. The counselor stated something I'll never forget and I treasure this truth in my heart for always. "The baby is a blessing, fornicating was the sin, Go and sin no more". I did not have premarital sex again. I was grateful for that Grace and not ashamed. Her words gave me the power to hold my head up high and walk past any clouds or thoughts of judgment, even if those were only in my mind. It was important to my fiance that the baby be born under the covenant of marriage and have his last name so I agreed to skip the one-on-one counseling and get married. HUGE mistake!! We by-passed God's covering and protection and that would have saved my naive heart a ton of heartache and pain. I walked down the aisle with a beautiful baby boy baking inside of me seven months pregnant. I was beautiful and glowing with friends and family celebrating and supporting us. Parked outside of the church was my wedding gift. It was a brand new white Land Rover truck with a huge red bow waiting for me. The devil really knows how to get us distracted by dangling treats in our pathway causing us to pay attention to things that cannot keep a marriage together. In that short cut, I cut short the character questions that would have been presented in the one on one counseling sessions. Those would have been administered through a seasoned, wise, and older minister. I will spare the painful details of that past life, I will just state that everything that a man should NOT do to his wife happened in the first 2 years of marriage. Our choices are long lasting and life changing.

The boys and I moved out in year six for six months and then again and for good in year eight. That marriage was not quickly dissolved . In the midst of the divorce I was far from perfect and THAT process took 3 years. During those three years of separation I began to spend time with a long time friend that I trusted and loved and although I tried to find comfort there; The Lord spoke very clearly "He can't fix what's broken inside, only I can heal your heart" Tears burst from my belly. I wasn't trying to cry but they came on like a flood.

I decided to do some work on me. I took two twelve week classes during the separation at two different churches that forced me to see myself. Raw and naked, I saw that I repeated the same mistakes from MY past. I had sex without being married. The mistake will be repeated until the lesson is learned. Although my sons father and I attended premarital classes and he had purchased and given me the ring, I chose to shortcut the process and forego the one on one counseling that was put in place for all couples at the church we attended. We completed the twelve months of pre-marital classes but since I got pregnant during the classes, we chose to get married and not attend the one on ones. The truth was I really didn't want to remain a single mother. I really wanted to get married and I loved him and thought that he loved me back. Short cuts often lead to disaster, especially spiritual short cuts. Hidden truths would have come up and come out in those one-on-one sessions. I have learned that God knows best and he doesn't need my assistance. He only requires my obedience and trust.

Here I was. I saw myself as I looked in the Word. I was raggedy and repeating the same mistake. Dang! I failed again! Oh, I was hard on people but I spared no self inflicting degrading words and thoughts on myself. I was the worst. I didn't deserve Grace. So I thought. When you know better you do better. I had been growing in Christ, and I SHOULD have known better. I couldn't blame THAT on him. I had to own my stuff. I wasn't perfect and I was paying a hefty price for my short cut and disobedience. Putting confidence in this flesh is dumb, but we all know that hindsight is 20/20. That divorce was from hell but so was the abuse I endured for the sake of my sons and a deep desire to kill the past generational curse of divorce on both sides of our family lines. A true ripping apart of the flesh but not just ours. Our sons took serious blows. They came to court several times, along with mutual friends, family members and neighbors. Just awful. The devil was after my seed. I know why! My sons are ALL blessed and highly favored and will change their generation. I bless God for the lessons. I bless God for revealing to me that I could never walk out my journey in perfection nor would I ever be deserving of his gift of Grace. So, He decided to shower on me and display his Grace and Mercy. Those unmerited gifts were chasing me down. I was a school teacher and the Lord opened every door and allowed me to have favor with every principal. Although my teaching license had expired (during the years I was a stay at home mom - teaching my younger sons) since I taught Spanish and was highly sought after by parents from my previous years of teaching, my name was on the classroom door with a provisional teaching license EVERY SINGLE year during that dreadful divorce. How many of you know that FAVOR is better than money! After teaching kindergarteners all day I was taking grad classes in the evening, then preparing meals and doing homework with my sons after night classes. On top of that I bless God for my village! I had a STRONG village who not only came to court countless times, but prayed, paid and did whatever was necessary to ensure me and my boys did not fall under all those spiritual and natural battles. Jesus kept me, forgave me, and in the pitch blackness of my future, he allowed me to put one foot in front of the other. By the time I was 32 both of my parents were deceased. I didn't have them to run to and bury myself in the comfort and safety of their homes, wisdom and love. That's why the Lord made my village so strong. Oh, how I love Jesus.

I TRUSTED God more than anyone and although he speaks gently, when God spoke these four words it changed the trajectory of my life. "The abuse is over" is what he spoke and after that no one's voice or opinion mattered. God hates divorce and He changes not. He didn't change that principle for me. However, he spoke so clearly that I had a peace that passed all natural understanding. I knew in my spirit that He would forgive me for the divorce. I didn't just "go through those valleys, I GREW through them." God taught me who I was IN HIM and I learned to hear his voice. Everyone around me from my children, my friends and even my ex husband knew that God spoke to me. I learned to trust in the Lord with ALL my heart and lean not on my own understanding. Yeah, though I walk through the valley of the shadow of death, I will fear no evil. I had indeed walked through the valley but God promised to never leave me and He was faithful and just. He never left me. He spoke to me clearer than ever. I learned to listen and trust HIM more than any living breathing human. His spirit would speak to my spirit which became my guide. Even if the person I was speaking to told me otherwise, I learned to ALWAYS trust God's voice. He never lies to me. In fact, He would cc me on everything concerning my household. My sons would always say "Mom has spidey senses! How would she know that" and I would correct them by stating it's the Holy Spirit! He's the "Truth Giver" so even if you lie, he'll tell me. The revealer! Oh, how He loves me! Then he gently reminded me that he loved me and spoke to me BEFORE I loved him. Yes, HE spoke to me back in the abortion clinic. He loved me and my seed. I never experienced THIS kind of Love.

The truth may hurt but it sets you free. You cannot operate or make decisions based on lies. The word of God says lying lips hates those it hurts. So, I always ask my sons to tell me the truth. I may be sad, I may cry, but speaking the truth means you love me too much to lie to me. I LOVE the truth!! My closest relationships are those that are laced in truth and the Lord always makes sure his daughter knows. After 19 years, countless court battles, many unseen scars and bruises, my ex husband and I are friends. I want him to be blessed and I strive to walk in kindness and love towards him. It is not always easy but when I look back at where the Lord has brought me from I know we paid a hefty price. Our choices are long lasting and life changing and they always affect more than us. Sin and unforgiveness cost us all and we pay some hefty prices. We lost money and some relationships. Oh we paid.. our health, our mind, our body and the priceless gift of Peace. We are a trinity like our heavenly Father. Our soul, body and mind will be affected by our choices whether healthy or toxic. If you have been divorced or going through a divorce, I challenge you to ask for forgiveness. I did. Even if you didn't do anything directly to destroy the marriage. We all have shortcomings and bring some damaged areas of our own lives into the union. Apologizing pleases God and proves that you belong to Him. It's liberating and it sets a prisoner free....YOU!

Single Again

(Larry)

S ingle, only one, not one of several. We are all single individuals, until you are in a relationship of any kind, and then we must govern ourselves accordingly. When you join a team you join with whatever skill set you developed up until that point in your life. Team means that you add your skills and abilities to the group to make something bigger, better, and stronger than you ever could on your own. In sixth grade my mother let me play on my first organized team, flag football. I played with my best friend at the time, Kevin who lived in the apartment above us in Suitland, Maryland. We were one of the top teams because he and I had been playing together on our neighborhood team for a long time. We developed a deeper knowledge of one anothers moves and strengths. I believe that gave us an advantage over some of the other teams we played and set a foundation in me being a great teammate on all the teams I would be a part of from then on. Playing on organized teams definitely teaches life lessons. What a team doesn't do is take away who you are as an individual. It is up to you to sharpen your skills and put in the work to improve yourself as a player. Each time you hit the field, you make a choice each day to give the best of yourself for the betterment of the team. When a teammate chooses to be an individual on a team failure is imminent.

Marriage is one of the toughest TEAMS you will ever be on because it is a lifelong commitment to an imperfect person. This person you choose is always changing and evolving and you are also always learning them, as if learning about yourself wasn't hard enough. Looking back on the circumstances leading up to me deciding it was time to get married was not well thought out. It was impulsive, filled with emotion and most of all selfish. I did not think about all that marriage entails. First of all, it takes two willing individuals and because I had already stepped on the gas with the proposal I overlooked her hesitation because she said yes. Marriage is a forever commitment, you know that part of the vows that says "till death do your part" Yeah, that one. I realized that this phrase can be literal and figurative. Actual physical death, but also death of the emotional attachment. We began our marriage with several significant differences. I was eight and half years her senior and we thought differently about a lot of things. Our belief system which is a major foundation was completely different. Although I was not where I am now as a Christian, I allowed non Christian beliefs to be at the forefront of our home. We had a different mindset regarding the finances. I paid all of our household bills, our wedding, lavish honeymoon, and several out of the country dream vacations. Meanwhile, although she was in school and bartending, she managed to have a secret stash and a separate savings. The motto I learned that she lived by was" what's yours is mine and what's mine is mine". These things aided our divorce but none more than the long distance we adopted with her travel to New Jersey several days a week and my travel back and forth to Maryland for work. During the last year we were together before we separated we disagreed a lot. They were all on major topics, such as children, refinancing and our next steps as a family. The fact that our foundation was not built on solid ground and God was not part of our lives our relationship gradually crumbled. She filed for divorce in 2007 for irreconcilable differences. We separated for two years which was the requirement in Pennsylvania. I have learned that patience, communication, and sacrificial love are the top three ingredients that entail a good marriage. Without one of them your dish is pretty much ruined. I only had two positive role models for a healthy marriage in my immediate family. However, not many details were shared in terms of manhood and leadership so I ended creating my own blueprint. I am a mama's boy true to heart. My mom had been my everything. She was my mom, dad, example for a mate and life teacher. Although, there are a few things we must discover on our own, the absence of my father had me striving to learn to be a man from the age of seven.

Our marriage lasted five years on paper, a total of nine. From the moment I received the divorce decree, I had to deal with the fact that I was single again. Spending the night at moms became the norm even though I still owned my own home in Pennsylvania. I was adjusting and processing what I thought was failure, and vowed to myself to never marry again. I was certain I would hold myself to that truth.

Begin Again

(Monet)

Stainless steel appliances, hardwood floors, tiny two bedroom apartment, 10 minutes away from my former 5,000sq ft home racked with bittersweet memories, but now I have something money can't purchase, PEACE! I'll take it. I moved into our new place, purchased 2 twin sized beds for my younger boys ages eight and six (one of my older sons was off to college and the other elder son stayed back by choice to finish out his senior year) I put a small wooden cross on the wall and that was our home for the next four years. It was perfect for me and my boys in every way. It was 10 minutes up the boulevard, 10 minutes from their father's house, 7 minutes from the elementary school where I worked and in the same community where all of my children's friends lived.

In our tiny two bedroom apartment I learned just how much God loved me. My faith was tested regularly. However, when God is all you have, you will learn that He is all you need. Also, being alone and quiet, I could hear him. I mean really listen to him and hear when the Holy Spirit spoke. Then I chose to do some work. I rolled up my sleeves and allowed the Lord to do some heart surgery on me. He led me to attend classes called Divorce Care at one local church and they also had divorce care for kids. It was perfect. Healing is a choice and available but it is a process. The classes I took were 12 weeks long but it was worth it! Each lesson and topic addressed a different issue or wound that resulted from the fracture of divorce. The adult classes were held right down the corridor from where my boys sat. The children's classes and videos matched the same lessons that we were taught in the adult classes. The leaders of the children classes were adults whose parents had been divorced so during the topic discussions, when and if the children chose to share, those leaders were able to listen with understanding because they had experienced the same emotions of frustration, disappointment, neglect or grief. These priceless jewels enabled the boys and I to deal with emotions that were hard to express and articulate during that season of deep disappointment and shattered dreams.

God got into those deep crevices of my heart and life that had me revisit my broken childhood. I brought baggage and deep wounds from my past into that marriage that he was not equipped to fix or heal. I was holding onto unforgiveness towards my mom for not saving herself which made me grow up too soon. I was still angry at my mother's ex-husband who molested me. Yeah, I opened my heart and mind to the truth that I wasn't perfect in the marriage. These lessons were blessing me and stretching me. Each weekly lesson was laced in the truth of God's word. The children's topics were the same as the adults. They just ministered on their level and accompanied with videos.

Topics like anger, fear, disappointment, forgiveness, grief and faith were all addressed and handled with such loving care. The classes and facilitators were priceless offerings of love and healing that we needed at that time. My heart is eternally grateful, but I had to do the work. The church was far, my ex-husband was resistant to any and everything I wanted to do for our boys if it wasn't on "my time" but I pressed on. Each class required study time, reflection and personal homework or "heart work" after each lesson. I could feel the layers of unforgiveness shedding. Whew, it was painful but I was growing and changing. The Word of God will change you, if you let it. Yield, submit, surrender all sound weak, but under God's loving care, you come forth changed, better, stronger;...healed. Healing takes time. Becoming mature in Christ is a lifelong process, but it requires TIME with the Father. If you don't give Him time to develop your character, mature and grow up in Him before you get married, at some breaking point you WILL give him your time during or after. It could be the loss of a parent, a child, or a deep disappointment in the marriage, but if you're HIS child, he wants you. All of you. It's so much wiser to give and get that quality time with God BEFORE you marry. When we spend time with the Father we learn who we are in His eyes and then if you don't measure up to someone else's standard it's okay to let them go with dignity and peace, because you already have your identity in Him. Hindsight is 20/20. When you know who you are, everything changes.

In Singleness we ought to learn who we are in Christ, but when we short cut that process we end up looking for someone to complete us, and fill us up, or build us up and that's not fair. It's not their job. I cut short my process. We ought to be whole BEFORE we get married not NEEDING anyone to complete us. My ex-husband was eight years older than me and I admired his drive and intellect. I thought because he had been saved for a long time and knew the bible better than me that he was a mature Christian. I was too young in the Word to know how to fruit inspect. He wasn't mature but he was successful so it was easy for him to hide behind his degrees and money. I was immature in the Word, not whole, had a damaged childhood and the "biggie" I did not know who I was from God's perspective. Therefore, I had unrealistic expectations and I allowed mistreatment. He couldn't give me what he didn't have and he had his own childhood wounds. When two people get married with these dynamics we will depend on our mate to give something they can not. They are human and will eventually fall short of our expectations or just flat out get tired of trying to fix our broken childhood wounds, scars and hurts. Of which I had a ton. If they also had a marred past that's a recipe for disaster, and we know that like spirits are drawn to one another. The brokeness in you attracts the brokeness in him.

So, there we have it. Two broken people trying to fix and repair each other and neither are qualified. Far from it. We end up hurting one another with criticisms, judgments, and add to that a heaping dose of impatience. A big painful mess. If we sprinkle two or three children in that mixture the cake will fall for certain because it's spilling into the next generation. They learn toxic and unhealthy communication skills and the cycle continues. Only the manufacturer can repair with original factory parts, thereby "restoring" what he created. We need God and He wants to come in and sup with us, but he's a gentleman. He won't bust the door down, he will knock. So he waits until we CHOOSE to let him in. This valuable time of quiet and solitude while in my tiny two bedroom apartment was necessary to heal and grow. At this point in my life it was time to grow. I am a teacher and an avid learner. I love to learn. Change was here. It was time to execute and implement. All of the classes and inner work helped my heart to heal, without leaning on any friend or man. This personal work allowed me to truly begin again.

Yellow Brick Road

(Larry)

Anyone that thinks they know how God operates, knows He loves it when you say what you are not going to do. For five years I was settling into a single life, that was going to be full of traveling and time spent finding out what I wanted out of life. No serious commitments just dating with no verbal promises. I was done with married life! One and done! I tried, it didn't work, now back to your regularly scheduled program. All of that just meant, I had prepped my younger self that marriage was going to be a one time thing. I was doing everything I set out to do, until one day in January 2010, my internal garmin started re-calculating, I was at mom's house, as usual when she asked me when I was going to get the rest of my, as she describes it, JUNK out of her house. She was referring to old memorabilia and a few other items stored in her basement, from dear ole A&T. There was a chest I started rummaging through that was with me since freshman year 1985. Inside was a yearbook, papers, cards, and letters I received during my time in college. I came across a piece of paper that was a class schedule, that showed classes that I knew I had not taken. I realized this couldn't be mine, and at the top of the paper read Monet Sanders. Well, I hadn't seen her since she left A&T, at least 20 plus years ago. I wondered to myself what she might look like now, because back in the day she was a tenderoni. How in the world did her schedule end up in my stuff? Well, facebook was now going to do the leg work of my curiosity. I typed her name in the search bar and got nothing, I went to her cousin Daryl's page again nothing. My last ditch effort was her cousin Deidra..ding ding ding we have a winner!. Her name was Monet Love, so it appeared she had been married at some point and time, however there was no evidence that this was the case now. I knew she was from N.Y. but she was living in the DMV area, so I decided I would send her a message to see if I could catch up with her, but I got no response. So I forgot about it. Fast forward exactly one year later in January 2011, I sent another message, again no reply. I thought maybe she was in a relationship, like she was in college, and that might be the reason she didn't reply, or she just didn't remember me because so much time had passed. I left it alone and went on about my business. There was something about January, even more there was something about the year 2012. January 2012, my paternal grandmother passed away. She and my grandfather were married 72 years and they were the rock solid foundation of our family. This was once again a life changing season in my life.

I was once again at moms looking at pictures and 'lo and behold' I found a picture of Monet and I posing together. I thought surely when she sees this picture, she will know who I am, and respond to my messages. It was late February while sitting with my grandfather, my phone rings and there is an unfamiliar voice on the other end, and a lot of background noise.

Monet had finally called. This was a conversation full of reminders of the past, only I was the only one that remembered. She filled me in on who she was and asked me if I knew Jesus all in the same breath, at least that is what it seemed like to me. Our conversation was brief but we spoke about three times that day, because she was on the baseball field cheering for her sons as they played in their little league game. It was March and I was on my way to South Carolina to play golf all weekend with my golf buddies. Monet and I spoke and decided this was a good time to meet up since I was passing by where she lived. Starbucks was the spot we would see each other for the first time in 22 years. We must have talked for four hours sitting in my car. We both may not have been looking at this encounter as a date or anything else, but it turned out to be our Yellow Brick Road.

OBEDIENCE Brings a Reward

(Monet)

February 2012 I saw Larry's facebook message. This old friend of mine remembered me from college at NCA&T but I could not remember him..at all. He reached out to me two prior times on facebook but I never saw it. Thank you Mr. Mark Zuckerberg. When I finally saw it I first thought "I can't meet some stranger on the internet" He's a stranger, he could be a killer. So, I made a few phone calls. I needed to do a background check. I did that by calling two of my cousins who also attended A&T with us. My cousin DT said that he was the nicest guy I ever met and my cousin Shae remembered us hanging out and dancing with him and remembered nothing but wonderful things. We met for a short time at a local Starbucks and spoke for about two hours. Two weeks later we spoke again. However, our first time together was actually a high intensity zumba class and this man actually got on the stage with me and danced. What! He can dance and this spontaneous fun was infectious! He didn't ask me out. We would speak on the phone and then decide okay well let's get together. Second date was a movie date with my brother. We dropped him off after the movie and then the two of us spent hours at Friday's talking, listening and getting to know one another. Third date was to see Joel Osteen. The title of his message was "Destiny Moments" nothing happens by accident. We looked at one another as we sat in my little buggy and knew that something was happening. I think in our next conversation I told Larry that I did not want to be intimate with him and that I wanted to get to know him without that element clouding our communication. He was such a gentleman and said "I haven't done that before but I'm willing to wait". Time would reveal if this was game or if he was sincere.

"What is your ring size? " Stop playing. You said you didn't want to get married again" I wasn't looking to get married, I was looking for the right person." He was respectful of my request of the sexual boundaries but with this new request, I told him that I needed him to meet my father in the Lord and my big brother in Christ. His response was "when do I meet them?" Six months into our courtship he asked my sons for my hand in marriage. They loved him and they were my world.

This was the start of our love story. My version of the narrative that has brought my King and I to this point. Here we are, eight years later and we feel like time flew. We have a beautiful marriage, (it's real with normal marital disagreements) a beautiful family, and a lovely home where each room is filled with rare and precious gems called laughter and love. We both have what we prayed for which is a loving marriage, where we are respected and treasured by our best friend and we place no one above one another. Priceless! I know I am tasting heaven on earth and **I THANK THE LORD** eachand every day for sending Larry to find me. Yes, it may sound cliche-ish but he literally "searched" for me on facebook and continued reaching out until I responded. I thank God he didn't give up because I truly never saw it until the right time.

Larry was looking through a box of memorabilia from college and found my college schedule mixed in his papers. So, he decided to look on facebook and search for me. In 2008 when my eldest son graduated and flew off to college in California I decided to get a fb page just so I could "look and see" what Monty was doing and posting. Once I realized that he would maintain his same integrity 3000 miles away I rarely got on fb. God makes no mistakes and HIS timing is perfect! Mr. Peterson reached out once in 2010, once in 2011, and once again in 2012 and I saw it that time! Why did I say God's timing was perfect?, because I was fighting and battling the devil in court against my ex-husband those prior years and our divorce was final in 2011. I probably did not have the time to even look at fb because I was representing myself in more than half of our court battles. Whew, what a painful season, but I grew tremendous FAITH through each and every trial. On top of that I began dating a college friend who was a great guy but after hearing God say "no" in one of my quiet moments, I obeyed that voice I knew would never misguide me. I was learning to listen and obey. That wasn't easy and court wasn't easy but Our God is Mighty in Battle and hears the prayers of his children.

The Word says in Isaiah 1:19 If you are willing and obedient you will eat the best of the land. I can truly say that we don't have the biggest house or the finest cars but we have the BEST marriage because our hearts and home are filled with tons of LOVE. We try our best to lavish love onto one another every single day, beginning with daily prayer together. We also fast together weekly and watch God move mightily. Then we choose to walk those prayers out by putting "feet" to our faith extending to our children, friends and family.

Obedience brings a reward and I truly believe that my husband and I have been rewarded. We waited to be intimate and REALLY got to know one another without jumping in the bed. We actually did jump. Instead of jumping in the bed we chose to "lock souls" or consummate our commitment to one another by jumping out of a plane together. YES! We went skydiving. We called it jumping out of our past into our future. We jumped out of fear and into fatih. That was one of my husbands bucket list things to do and he had never done it. So, after he asked my sons for my hand in marriage I called the closest skydiving location and set our appointment. It was awesome! I am not adventurous at all, but I am all for doing something spiritual which helped us stay committed to our plan. We wore shirts that I made that read "Trust God" and that is exactly who we believed brought us together at this perfect divine time.

Since it was both our second marriages, I wanted to experience some "firsts" with the love of my life whom I know that God sent looking for me. We had a beautiful engagement party, a first for us both. It was hosted by one of my sisters in Christ and my best friend. At the party we played the video of us skydiving. Up to that point only two people knew about it, so a room filled with our closest friends and family watched in amazement as they experienced us ascend in a plane and descend with a parachute. It was so thrilling as each person felt our love for one another. To top off that magical night, the Lord sent a dove to my sister's house that day. The dove posed and took a picture with us and left the next morning. The dove represents peace and love and indeed we feel God's peace and love surrounding our marriage.

I also had another first, a bridal shower. My sister Donna lavished her love on me and I felt every drop of it. She was my maid of honor and my trusted confidant. The bridal shower was absolutely perfect. Classy atmosphere, food, laughter and games, and the afternoon closed with a liturgical dance performed by a local church group that I love. They danced to the song "It's Working" - This is my season, for Grace, for Favor, This is my season, to reap what I have sown. I cried tears of joy because I believe every lyric for my life. I always did it my way, however, when I did life the way God designed I quickly saw the benefits and blessings. Our God is a God of second and third and fourth, and so on chances. You feel me? His Grace and Mercy never run out and I am so grateful. I was finally striving to live His word AND I had a partner who was willing at the age of 45 to walk with me, learn from Godly men, treat me like a queen, and without changing who he was, be a Godly example for my sons to emulate. Yes, my sisters! I am truly walking in Grace. I am a living example that God does not give up on us. I've been taught the Word of God by awesome men of God and although I had knowledge of the Word and experienced God's love for me, I still flunked many tests. But God! He is faithful and gave me another test. The guilt and shame that follows disobedience and the pain that one experiences as a believer when you have let God down is just not worth it. I want to hear God say, "well done my good and faithful servant". So, I keep pressing. Striving to please God and encourage others to see His goodness is my daily mission. It's our family mission statement. We are, because He is! Our Goal is to make God look good not ourselves. Obedience indeed brings a reward and I am living my BEST life. Just when I didn't think life could get any sweeter, the reward was a few faith steps away…

Love at first sight

(Larry)

In less than five minutes into a conversation anyone can see Monet expresses goodness, kindness, joy and love to those she is around. There is an aura she gives off that is infectious. I wasn't looking for anything except a reconnection with an old friend that I had a crush on in college, that lived in the area, so I thought. After returning from my golf trip, two weeks had passed since we spoke. She wanted to know how my trip was, and this was something I wasn't expecting. I thought she was with someone, and I was free and dating. I was just honest about not wanting a commitment. She was interested in hooking me up with one of her girlfriends, but she said that wouldn't work because I was not looking to get married again. The thought of getting married again had passed and in my rear view mirror. Somehow we got to the point of setting up a date for a movie because she didn't want to go by herself, however, I was working, so I took a raincheck. It took some time because she lived on the baseball field at her sons' games but we eventually got around to that date. I believe the movie was Hunger Games, and her brother came along. Then she invited me to her Zumba class. She obviously forgot what her cousin Shaelafa told her about me, during her background check of me. I was a dancing machine. Shoot she didn't know, I wasn't going to tell her, but she was about to find out. After that day several dates followed, to the zoo, comedy club, dinner and a movie. None of our get togethers stood out like Fridays. That's where we almost shut the restaurant down talking and learning a lot about one another. Then there was the date with Joel Osteen. My entire family was there. The date and the message was unforgettable. Directly following I was supposed to be taking her to her car when something came over us. We were looking at one another without saying a word, but I could hear her loud and clear. It was the weirdest feeling I think I've ever had. I could see her for who she was, and it felt like Love at first sight.

We spent so much time around each other, it felt as if we were a couple even though we weren't. There was no sex going on, yet I didn't want to be anywhere else. I realized that is the only true way to find out if you really like someone. Too many people think sex is the way to keep someone interested. Or they believe that if they are intimate with their partner, that entitles them to a relationship. When you have sex early, all that does is set a craving for more sex, and sets the basis of your relationship. Remember what you start off doing in a relationship sets a precedence, and you have to keep it up in order to keep them. Waiting breaks down facades, it also gives you better satisfaction in your relationship, by enhancing what you already love about them. After a while I wanted to only see her. So that meant I had to notify whoever else I was dating, which turned out to be a tougher conversation than I thought, but I knew what was happening between us was something different. Something special. Everyday was different, from baseball games, to jumping out of airplanes, we even competed how to "out give" one another. In my previous relationship I had God on the back burner of my life, and He wanted the spotlight. Once He took his rightful position in my life, everything became clearer. I know I said I wasn't looking to get married again, I was looking for the right person in my life. In August of 2012 I asked Monet her ring size? Her reply was," stop playing with me". I wasn't playing, I knew this woman was special to me, and I didn't want to lose her. Because Monet's parents were both deceased, she had me meet the men that filled that void in her life, both Ministers, her brother from another mother Campbell, and her Father in the Lord, Minister Harris. I made it a priority to ask her sons for her hand, since they were the protectors of her happiness. On 12/12/12 friends and family came to witness our worlds become one.

London- Our Answered Prayer

(Monet)

The one thing that is constant in life is change. When I turned 40 I said to all of my friends, I am locking my hair and tying my tubes. I love to wear my hair in a variety of styles and locks are so permanent. So, although I loved the look I changed that declaration. Then I went through a divorce. So, I changed my mind on tying my tubes. What if I remarried someone with no children and they wanted to try? I was still open to having more children. I love children. So, I pressed the pause button on both and didn't change my hair or body. The Lord was preparing to grant me a strong desire suppressed from long ago. This gift from God was truly special that would bless all of our worlds. He needed to get a special little princess delivered and I was chosen to be her mommy.

My husband is such a kind and loving spirit he gently and warmly said that not only could he marry me with four sons but that he would love everything and everyone attached to me.

It was genuine and sincere, and it was also tested and passed. He stood by my side as I battled for things promised in my former marriage. Larry didn't even flinch. That madness lingered into the first few years of our marriage. Crazy don't stop being crazy, but God is bigger and more powerful than all the fiery darts from the enemy and tests the heart of man. Larry would need to forgive my ex because we had children together and we would have many events that would require us all being together, in peace. Larry chose to forgive him. My sons witnessed it, our families witnessed it, but God was also watching. Thank God that season was over.

I quietly prayed. "Lord Jesus, please strengthen my womb and allow me to bring at least one baby from my belly to bless this man." It was earnest and heartfelt. Then I went to the doctor. I was 43 years old and I had been pregnant many times, more than the number of children I bore. I never had an abortion, but miscarried three times in between sons. So, I needed to see what the doctors would say about my body. Bed rest, cervical cerclage, and all types of different procedures might be necessary, but for my King, I was willing to try, pray and believe that my body, heart and mind could endure and carry the gift of life one more time. After a wave of tests, the report came that I was just above the level of having a low egg count. So, we immediately tried IVF. Our insurance paid 100% for three pregnancies with live births. Hot diggity! First round, I did not get pregnant, but the second time I did, and had extra fertilized eggs. Science is amazing and

I bless God for the process and their wisdom. But the process PROVED even more that God is real and that HE alone is in control for every baby born. The big days of egg retrieval, and then fertilization, and final step of the embryo transfer of the eggs was ALL evidence that God must be involved. The sweet doctors and nurses wished and said good luck, because they knew that ultimately, they were not in control. Somewhere in the dark space of the prepared uterus, the fertilized and developing embryo will either lodge into the uterus wall or not. Science can not fix or determine this outcome. This is 100% if God says yes! Their only instructions were to look for signs of pregnancy; throwing up, nausea, or any other outward signs. We knew this was a faith walk and God does his best work in the dark.

A few weeks later I was pulling over to the side of the road throwing up anything I ate for breakfast. I have never thrown up in any pregnancy. This must be a girl. Our sweet button had me earling for 3 months, then making several trips to the ER because she was kicking, twirling and pushing down on my cervix causing frequent bleeding. Then at 28 weeks my water broke. Didn't this little mama know that this is a forty week journey? Oh well, my doctor announced instead of me being in the hospital for two months, she would be taking her today. Today! Okay, let me wrap my mind around all these immediate changes. Wait, no you can't. Am I ready? Upon her next check of the baby's heartbeat, the doctor snatched the cords out of the wall, rushed me down the hall closing the door in my husband's face. He would not be in the room nor would he cut the umbilical cord. As unfortunate as that was, our doctor saved London's life. Her heart rate dropped so she made the quick wise decision to take her out now! They got her pretty little self out in three minutes. One minute to knock me out, one minute to cut my stomach and one minute to lift her out and suction her mouth and nose. What a journey we had!

This strong senorita with her sweet "Loli" self was 2 pounds and 2 ounces and feisty. Each day she got stronger and stronger. We had a row of books that her brothers read each time they came to visit her in the hospital. Our princess couldn't be discharged before she reached certain critical goals. She was breathing on her own now and each day making strides. She tried to breastfeed and was able to latch on, but my milk wouldn't come in since she arrived so early. I was able to breastfeed all of my sons and I know that was best for babies. THIS was a "first" that I was not enjoying. So, the bottle and similac it was. We had our eye on the prize. Can't cry over spilled milk when God allowed this miracle to occur. Next, removing her breathing tube and then feeding tube. Whoohooo, we were cruising and had grown to 5.2 pounds by the time we were discharged from the hospital. We each wore a supergirl, superwoman, and superman shirt to ascend on our flight out of the hospital. We were ready to leave and pop that popsicle stick! We were on our way, flying high with little London Monet, our sweet little love package in tow!

God allowed her to enter the world one week before my husband's birthday and Father's Day. It was indeed an early birthday present. She is spunky, sparkly and everything girly. My sister tells me that I used to ask her to keep all of my nieces pretty dresses and clothes because I felt that one day I may have a daughter. I had so many sons (even the children that I miscarried were three boys) I had forgotten those requests. But God! He did not forget and YEARS later, in a new marriage, with a new mate, in a new home, and completely NEW LIFE, He granted that desire of my heart. She is everything I could have ever asked or hoped for in a daughter. She brings out the best in all of her brothers and lights up our entire home. She is such a compassionate soul and never wants anyone to hurt. She came here wanting to heal and help. She says to her Dad the firefighter, "Daddy I will be a doctor when I grow up so that when you bring sick people to the hospital I can see you and help them!"

What a beautiful journey to London my life has been, and the journey has just begun.

London- Our Answered Prayer

(Larry)

I knew as a kid that I always wanted a big family with lots of kids, but I had no clue how God would do that especially after I divorced. I just loved the feeling of being around lots of family and I admired those that had lots of siblings. Although it was just my sister and I, we always spent time with cousins that were like our siblings. I had no idea what God had in store for me, knowing I wanted a big family. I didn't have any kids in my first marriage, and after that dissolved, clearly I was never going to have any children at all, so I thought. When I remarried I gained four wonderful sons, Daniel, Joshua, Monty, and Abiy. At age 45 and my wife 43, our youngest son was 9 and the oldest was 24. There we were having full conversations of trying to have a baby together. This was indeed a joy with just the possibility. I had no idea we would be talking about having a baby. I was excited about the possibility of having a child. I was also taken aback that my wife was willing to put herself through a pregnancy at her age.

She knew there was a reason she hadn't closed up shop. So we started trying, and when nothing happened for several months, we started researching IVF. We found everything we needed and got started right away. I can't tell you how excited I was through this process and the amount of prayers I said. The talking and music I played on my wife's belly. I gotta be honest, I screamed and cried a joyful tear at twenty weeks, when the doctor told us it was a GIRL. My wife was happy for me having my first child, and I was happier for her, that she would be having her first girl.

Everything was great in the Peterson household. That little momma wouldn't stay still in the belly, swimming from one side to the other, posing for the 4d camera. On June 6th 2014, I was on the golf course of all places Hole #15 when my son Monty called me and said Mom's water broke, and she was at the hospital. I was about 45 miles away. It took me one hour and 15 minutes to get there. We were right at 28 weeks and four days, the doctors told us Monet would be in the hospital until the baby was born. HUH? The baby's due date was Aug 27th. Whoa!!! I was trying to wrap my head around my wife being in the hospital for almost three months. Well, if she was going to be there, so was I. On Sunday June 8th, still waiting for the amniotic fluid to build back up, the baby's heart rate went down, the doctor gave a little stimulation and it came back up. The doctor told us if that happened again she would have to deliver. Somewhere around noon, which felt like an eternity, the doctor was out delivering other babies, when the heart rate went down again. She came in and started looking at the baby by sonogram, while we all stood quiet. Then without hesitation she called for a code Blue and started unplugging the bed, and putting on caps and gowns and gloves, and pushing the bed down the hallway with nurses coming out of rooms and doorways. I was hot on their heels, only to be stopped at the doors to the operating room, telling me I couldn't go any further. I was disappointed because I was so looking forward to cutting the umbilical cord and holding my child. Instead I waited anxiously outside those doors thinking and praying for my two ladies. The doors finally opened and out came three people dressed in scrubs pushing an incubator with my little lady inside. I was told my wife was being stitched up and she would be fine. My wife and I already discussed what I was going to do if they were separated, I was going with the baby wherever they were taking her. I was on the elevator with the baby headed to the NICU. When I finally got to my wife her condition wasn't the greatest after the trauma she just went through. She was throwing up bile and hunched over in pain. I wanted to trade places with her so desperately. She was only concerned about the baby's condition and when she could see her. The baby was fine. She had her own room and incubator. They were feeding her through a tiny tube in her nose that went to her stomach and there was a tiny ventilator covering her face. I was full of different emotions because it felt like she was still in Monet's stomach, the only difference was I could see her now. She was 2lbs 2oz and about 15 inches long. She was so tiny, so beautiful and mine. When her eyes opened my heart was engraved. I could not stop my tears from falling. I knew God had answered our prayers with London Monet Peterson.